W9-DEX-914

PROVINCETOWN POETS SERIES
first books by new poets

VOLUME VIII
Peter Saunders
My Father's Shoes

VOLUME VII
David Matias
Fifth Season

VOLUME VI
Ellen Dudley
Slow Burn

VOLUME V
Mairym Cruz-Bernal
On Her Face the Light of La Luna

VOLUME IV
Martha Rhodes
At the Gate

VOLUME III
Anne-Marie Levine
Euphorbia

VOLUME II
Michael Klein
1990

VOLUME I
Keith Althaus
Rival Heavens

MY FATHER'S SHOES

PROVINCETOWN POETS, VOLUME VIII

Series Editor: Christopher Busa

MY FATHER'S SHOES

Poems by Peter Saunders

PROVINCETOWN ARTS PRESS

ACKNOWLEDGMENTS

These poems first appeared, or will appear, sometimes in different form or different title, in the following publications; my thanks to them all.

Times Literary Supplement Poetry Competition (UK): "Cape Cottage in Winter"
The Eclectic Muse Anthology: "My Father's Shoes," "Cold Comfort"
The Longfellow Journal (Longfellow Society): "Perfect Fit," "My Himalayas,"
  "Oyster Pond"
Provincetown Arts: "Provincetown Birdsong"
The Aurorean: "Grow More Flowers," "Spring Hope"
Spectrum (Northeastern University): "Blind in P'town," "Bad News"
Provincetown Magazine: "Leaving Cape Cod," "Spring Hope"
WOMR-FM *Poetry Corner*: "Ask Any Frog"
Cape Codder: "The List Is Done"
Saltwind Millennium Anthology: "Stars," "Raccoon"
The Worcester Review: "Porcelain Tea Cup," "Relationships"
Prime Time: "First Light," "Back Seat Driver"
Reflections (Cape Cod Community College): "Nana," "Perfect Fit," "Cape Cottage
  in Winter," "Starry Night," "My Old Cracked Tune"
www.ragazine.cc: "Lois at Her Farmstand," "Aging"
Christian Science Monitor: "Winter Squirrel"

Copyright © 2010 by Peter Saunders. All rights reserved. No part of this book may be used or reproduced in any manner without written permission, except in the case of brief quotations embodied in critical articles or reviews.

Provincetown Arts Press
650 Commercial Street, Provincetown, MA 02657
www.provincetownarts.org

Frontispiece by Linda Saunders
Book design by Irene Lipton

This book is funded in part by the Massachusetts Cultural Council, a state agency that also receives support from the National Endowment for the Arts.

Library of Congress Cataloging-in-Publication Data
    Saunders, Peter, 1934-
    My father's shoes : poems / Peter Saunders.
        p. cm. -- (Provincetown poets series ; v. 8)
    ISBN 0-944854-56-7 (alk. paper)
    I. Title.
    PS3619.A825M9 2010
    811'.6--dc22
                        2010009413

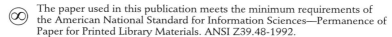

The paper used in this publication meets the minimum requirements of the American National Standard for Information Sciences—Permanence of Paper for Printed Library Materials. ANSI Z39.48-1992.

PRINTED IN USA
1 2 3 4 5 6 7 8 9 10

TO

Donald Baker who sparked my poetry
Liz Rosenberg who inspires sparks
Michael Klein who fans sparks to flame
Chris Busa who shapes the flame
My wife, Linda, whose art is poetry

CONTENTS

I

My Old Cracked Tune   PAGE 3
My Father's Shoes   4
Perfect Fit   5
Love Letters   6
Cold Comfort   7
Tenement on Joy Street   8
I Missed You   9
The House on Lincoln Street   10
Last Day of Childhood   11
Grandmother   12
Grandfather   13
Raspberries   14
Blame   15
First Death   16
Teddy   17
Faraway Friend   18
The End   19
Depression   20
Glimpses   21
Aromas   22
Nana   23

II

My Father's Briefcase   26
Ashes to Ashes   27
Goodbye   28
Ode to Al   29
Homeless Slim   30
Fantasy   31
Tragedy   32
Long Trek   33
Winter Squirrel   34

Oyster Bay   35
Starry Night   36
First Light   37
Inconveniences   38
Guys Who Piss Me Off   39
Costs   40
The Fool   41
Second Time Around   42
Harry   43
Savior   44
Grow More Flowers   45
Accusing Alan   46
Alan's Story   47
Endangered   48
Lois and Da   49
Lois at Her Farmstand   50
Parenting   51
Loraine-Walking   52
Provincetown Allows No Birdsong   53
Coping   54
Cape Cottage in Winter   55

III

Sagamore Beach   58
Communion   60
One fifteen p.m.   61
Jump   62
Three Spring Haikus After Surgery   63
A Couple of Cold Ones   64
Idle Thoughts While Healing   65
Arnold's Axiom   66
Thoughts on a Wedding in Provincetown   67

Bagel and Coffee at 6 a.m. on MacMillan Wharf   68
Old Colony Tap   69
Aging   70
Spring Hope   71
Gone Too Long   72
Able Seaman   73
Crossing Over   74
Triumph: Boston Marathon, April 15, 1996   75
Cape Cod   76
Day's End in Provincetown   77
Deliverance   78
Did I Make a Daughter-Difference?   79
Be Quick   80

INTRODUCTION

My Father's Shoes illustrates my life and my parents' lives merging back into significance after being ruptured by the Great Depression. My brief time with parents Paul and Katherine ("Patsy" to my father), six years of love, writing, and art, suppressed for decades, were enough to plant the seeds of what I now am—poet, teacher, writer, embracing my mother and father in death, as I never had the fortitude to possess them in life.

The first section describes the world as I found it as a child: grimy tenements, then a warm roof for fifteen years with frugal Yankee grandparents, visits to my father's penniless but joyous mother. The third section is my world in my eighth decade, blessed beyond comprehension by events I hardly grasp. The middle section attempts to bridge the unbridgeable. So much of what I've endured—divorce, life-threatening illness, near bankruptcy—has been supplanted by deep and lasting love, financial peace, and a poetic voice.

The initial focus of my poems was on my own life and lean times. This evolved into a growing comprehension of my parents' brief, hard, yet glorious years together, and their doomed love. My mother's letters from the love of her life, the father of her sons, survive to tell of their courtship. Of how wildly and foolishly they loved, with no money and no job. She begged disapproving parents for help. Her mother brought food to the tenement but her father wouldn't come, his Protestant prudence no match for a Catholic husband recklessly making babies with his manic-depressive daughter.

No matter that both young parents had talents meriting support. The poet James Elroy Flecker (1884–1915) had been my father's literary mentor back in the Cotswold town of Cheltenham, England, and later Paul had published a first novel (a mystery novel my parents thought would make them rich); Patsy was a budding poet. These meant nothing to a Maine farmer who had scratched wealth from city dirt.

When my younger brother, Richard, was born, the pressure mounted for my mother. *Come home and all is forgiven, but your man must go. No parental role, no lover. You haven't earned it. You're not responsible. A roof, food, clothes for your sons, but no love. Love is too much to ask when you're a lustful daughter costing us money.* A cruel choice that Patsy resisted for six years, moving from slum to slum: Joy Street, Carver Street, then Cambridge Street, tenements across from the Charles Street Jail in Boston; each dingier, dirtier, with jobs harder and harder to find. She beseeched her mother for *anything,* but to get more, Patsy must return home, leaving the only love she'd ever known; *that was the price.* Sons have so many needs, she was told. And, finally, for the sake of her sons, she agreed to leave Paul and move in with her unrelenting parents. Her younger son, not understanding, withdrew, unhappy and fearful.

I, being older, was sent from time to time to live with my other grandmother to save food, *and I blossomed.* A joyous widow, she walked me through parks to pick elderberries, then let me sip the wine she made. Mornings began with a *rooster* egg in my own egg-cup, followed by sewing lessons, and later on she taught me to dance. It was an early glimpse of *real* life, prying the lid open for a peek at what I now have, sixty years later.

I was a bit of a rolling stone in my middle years, achieving a degree in engineering, transitioning through two marriages, welcoming two beloved daughters (Lois and Loraine), and living in various residences in Maryland and Massachusetts. I finally found my true love, Linda, later in life along with my true vocation as a poet. My father remarried and we saw him from time to time as he went back and forth from England to America, checking in on his mother, visiting his children. Though he wrote the definitive history of Edward Jenner, MD, the developer of the smallpox vaccine (*Edward Jenner, The Cheltenham Years, 1795–1823;* University Press of New England, 1982), material success eluded him. He inevitably arrived in the States broke and needing our help. My mother, despite the trials of our early years, never gave up her creative work, self-publishing at least eight poetry chapbooks, and writing numerous magazine articles.

And yet, even now, never a day passes for me, without hearing my mother's sobs. Only now can I see, she is smiling through her tears.

My parents' creative legacy lives on in my sculptor-brother and in me, and through me, in my students. As a teacher of senior writers, I feel the thrill of my first poem replicated each time one of my elderly students creates a poem and has the courage to read it aloud. Both student and teacher, and the loved ones we write about, have acquired a voice.

MY FATHER'S SHOES

I

My name is Solomon Levi
the desert is my home,
my mother's breast was thorny,
and father I had none.

The sands whispered, *Be separate,*
the stones taught me, *Be hard.*
I dance, for the joy of surviving,
On the edge of the road.

— STANLEY KUNITZ
"An Old Cracked Tune"

MY OLD CRACKED TUNE

My name is Elroy Flecker,
        city tenements my home.
                Mother-love tenacious,

father ripped away,
        no money—nor job.
                Left only his shoes for

exploring gritty streets.
        Salvaged myself in the
                rubble but shoes commanded—

trudge on. Cobblestones echoed—
        be hard. Now I dance for the
                joy of tripping down the road.

MY FATHER'S SHOES

carry him over hurdles
he feels on entering in-laws' house
his poverty unwelcome here.
He loves me no less despite
sparse visits by trolley and foot.

Grandparent voices overhead mutter
workless means worthless.
Me at knee-level made uneasy,
my eyes drop to the floor
where squat his shoes,
creased with worry like the stubbled face
I'd just kissed.

His careworn Horween cordovans,
Depression wracked,
shined on banana peels
though cracked clean through,
soles brown and torn and separated
from each other, just like us.

PERFECT FIT

With pale gold curls, beauty that will last to her fifties,
she'll marry Harry her mother says, the nice American boy
while father favors Protestants,
families who own mills or presses or money.

Harry fits.

But a dark Englishman with Roman nose,
fresh off the boat from Southampton
is the man she seduces in a closet
off a lecture hall at Boston University. My father
reads poems of James Elroy Flecker:
I was a poet, I was young,
and writes love letters on wrapping paper
she'll save till death.

Father doesn't fit.

Years before my birth they even pick my names,
rejoicing at what naïve love conceives,
then marry without a dime between them.

My perfect fit.

LOVE LETTERS

My father's letters survive to tell of their
    courtship, how wild and foolishly they loved
        with no cash and no work. Mother implores her
            parents to help. Grandmother drives a new

Plymouth to the tenement with food. Grandfather won't
    come, his prudence no match for profligacy. Though
        father's first novel is published and
            mother's a promising poet,

promise means nothing to Maine farmers
    scratching wealth from city soil.
        Brother is born. For six years
            we move from slum to slum.

Joy Street   Carver Street   Cambridge Street.
    Each hovel dingier, jobs harder to find.
        Mother begs her mother
            for *anything*.

Starved out of marriage
    my mother abandons the only love
        she'll ever know, returns home for
            food, clothes, a roof for her sons.

COLD COMFORT

He's through the door—Salvation Army—striding
to the rear, winter coats, last rack on the right, five left,
strung like leaves on the limbs of a winter oak.

He   my father   grabs the heavy brown
with frayed cuffs.
Knows it fits.

She   my mother   slips in to try it
while he shivers in front of the A&P begging
with the HUNGRY sign.

Clutching three dirty bills, six quarters
and three dimes, he lays cash on the counter
noiselessly, eyes down.

Clerk counts   eyes him and nods.

Outside   knives of chill darkness slice her worn dress.

TENEMENT ON JOY STREET

Me immersed in
        soapy water, bathroom steamy,
                mirror dripping mist,
                        and mother standing naked
                                beyond the tub.

Bath water heated
        in a tall copper kitchen
                tank, shared by all,
                        one by one. Except
                                my brother's not yet born.

My slim mother is pregnant.
        I am less than three years old and
                she reads me bedtime stories.
                        Don't need to hear her say it to
                                know she loves me.

I MISSED YOU

no doubt about that.
The other guys had dads
to play catch with. Except
for a borrowed dad lent generously,

I had none.
And when we met
for a meal with brother in tow
it was never enough, I wanted more.

If it was hard on you,
alone, unloved and broke,
in that dark hole on Carver Street, why
leave only bits of you for me:

your Parker pen
bestowed on me
and later lost in haste.

A Rolls razor
to last a life,
yet you never saw me shave.

A sketch of ships in battle
drawn for my war worship.

My first birthday card
the year before you died.

These things I hold close
as a sailor clings to wreckage
after storms.

THE HOUSE ON LINCOLN STREET

A loft bedroom shared with brother Richard,
    never bedrooms of our own.
        Separate decrepit beds, often broken,
            grandparents nothing if not frugal.

A bench to build model airplanes—
    Grumman Avenger, Hellcat, Lightning—to
        do homework and write murder mysteries
        grandmother condemns.

A table we five eat at each night,
    gruff grandfather at the head, me at the foot,
        never a word passing between us.
            Trumpet lessons on a borrowed horn.

Top of the loft stairs, her sobs are audible.
    Mother, come home a beggar, a third child.
        Quiet tears shout louder from my childhood
        than all grandfather's cursing,

louder than praise teachers heap on me when I excel
    trying to prove I'm not as bad as my parents.
        What's a six-year-old to think,
            homeless under a borrowed roof?

LAST DAY OF CHILDHOOD

A small black & white photo on my wall
        is mute salute to lost youth. I'm nine,
                skinny ribs showing shorts no shirt.
                        Lanyard and whistle around my neck.

Not a care on this last day of childhood,
        leaving for Trinity Camp in an hour.
                Homesick for one year only. In
                        eight summers receive not one visit.

I'm on my own.
        Before that June
                I failed to notice what our forced move
                        to a borrowed roof meant.

Now, as an adult, it's starkly clear.
        My mother—
                now that my brother, she and I
                        live with her mother and father—

is demoted to child.
        Earning my getaway
                takes twelve years.
                        Mother never does.

GRANDMOTHER

At only nine or ten
my mystery story makes the
grandmother the murderer and you
my grandmother   pronounce the tale
terrible   for grandmothers

never murder   and I
        stop writing   for grandmothers
never lie   and I
        being only nine or ten
never guess your fear

that I may follow my parents' path,
be dead to you,
like your daughter and son-in-law
whose passions   with words   you murdered.

GRANDFATHER

I awoke from a dream this Sunday morning
      having laid my hands on yours at the dining table
            where we ate for years without speaking.
                  You looked at me with tears.

It took fifteen years for me to escape.
      Your daughter never did, nor you,
            your head hung low over ledgers.
                Did you return last night

to explain what you missed,
      cheating us both. Or to beg forgiveness
            hoarding words that might have fed my
                hunger. You who lived long but little.

My poor soil lacked nourishment yet
      you, Maine farmer, saw profit in winter wheat.
            My spring task was hard sweat with pitchfork then
                sowing seeds for summer harvest.

Now I lay hands on a poet with Parkinson's
      who blesses me despite my flaws and knows
            I'll be never perfect. Did I forgive you?
                My harvest is rich.

RASPBERRIES

If gray slacks and shirt,
floppy hat and hoe hide a passion,
it is these scarlet spheres so
unlike your stifled life.

A fling of wild abandon
—like love—requires attention.
You stake green sprigs atop mounds
of manure and wait for leaves

that first summer. Then weed and tamp
and trim until the second season when ruby
beauties burst to pluck, pop
and quench the driest life.

BLAME

You turned to me as we drove
        up Route 3 after Sagamore
                Beach day warmed the little feet of
                        children and grandsons.

Blurted out after decades,
        Your father
                couldn't support us so I
                        had to take you kids home to live

with my parents. I'm sorry.
        Like others in that Depression,
                you chose children over spouse
                        yet never a harsh word for my Da.

Heaped abuse on parents
        for not taking him in, too.
                Years later we found his love
                        letters—forfeiting happiness.

I'm not angry—
        I never knew.
                I wish I'd known—
                      I should have.

FIRST DEATH

Tommy Lynch. Eighth grade
begins without you that September
with teacher leaving your desk empty,
hoping you'll return.

You don't.

You don't play football in the cemetery
anymore either
in those baggy pants
kids from big families wear.

Saint Catherine's funeral, Norwood, Mass.

Six of us with white gloves I'll save forever
barely manage to carry you
on wobbly legs
the casket weight immortal.

TEDDY

Miss O'Sullivan's homeroom back row.

You're a T and I'm an S.
I get A's and sweat through the wrong college.
You're an older-wiser-taller
handsome footballer and sports giant
defending Pablo the bat boy

from bullies. You're a champ
long before you move into my flat
when I graduate and move south
with an engineering degree and wife
to father daughters and flunk corporate.

You mature to be a Norwood cop
raising four kids with Carol.
I miss you till our fortieth.
One last time to hear wisdom
from my high school hero,

telling me you bent the bastard
across the hood of a cruiser.
Warned him if he ever beat her again
you would break his knees and ever after
if I need a cop I'll wish it were you.

FARAWAY FRIEND

You are old shoes
slipped into easily
like an old love
despite days or years apart
for the safe comfort
of wiggling toes
without fear
after new leather's
pinched too tight.

Lucky us
have other pairs
in case you die
the rest cry.

THE END

is nothing
in a bar
dimly lit
round table
top greasy
under palmsweat
farthest corner
out of sight.

Parting,
the moment bound
stands starkly
in focus
like TV on overhead
with picture
no sound.

DEPRESSION

Were I a goldfinch
I'd make my wings your wings
fluff my feathers and lift you

when depression laid us low.
Just two yellow streaks
of up and down

trailing strings of song.
We'd rollercoaster
Prozac-free.

GLIMPSES

Full moon flirts
from behind clouds
dressing for a big night out.

Would that warm days
could be stored in a chest to
blanket the cold ones.

Wet snow turns trees to white lace—
no longer flat flakes—maples
become plump snowballs.

Each moment holds a life in its palm
whole and complete like a snowflake melting
no less perfect for its brevity.

AROMAS

My aunt Ruth always had time to fold me in her
powder-scented hugs. The nephew
without a full set of parents. She won me over

driving her Dodge like a trucker on vacation from
Cranston to Lake Champlain. Knew the places
to stop where chips came with a hamburger.

Never a better driver. Wellesley master of economics,
sixty-five years wife and mother. Her church
works at Providence Housing still bear her name.

A sizeable woman, she ordered a kitchen abuzz with holiday
preparation, as I stole morsels of turkey stuffing and pie
dashing through on that one precious day a year.

Thanksgiving at 76 Seaview Avenue
where my cold world warmed once and still does
with remembered aromas of Ruth.

NANA

Though dead twenty years
you're with me when I wake,
delighting that you're vivid still.
Broke, you are never broken but
rise again with that smile

sipping elderberry wine we made
from berries picked together.
After going blind you pop
strawberries stem and all and smack
your lips, near the end declaring
I cling to memories.

And promptly recall boy Brad
your one love who marched
from your England to the Boer War
in '98 never to return.
Tall with wavy hair—
in uniform—his missing picture
painted on your heart
beating you to the grave
by eighty-three years.

A life you might have had
except for a stray war long forgotten.
What those eyes saw of love
and death and disappointment . . .
three sons and daughter scattered,
a philandering husband who left you
penniless to cope with a century.

II

Tell me, what is it you
plan to do with your one wild
and precious life?

— MARY OLIVER

MY FATHER'S BRIEFCASE

He always arrived with the same scuffed leather case
borrowed from Danny, who let him flop for free
to be near the trolley line that took him to his Mama's
which is why he'd come penniless from England each year

for fear she'd die before he could scratch his way back.
It was all he brought to stay however long we put him up
dressed in the same sad shoes, white shirt, striped tie,
mismatched coat and pants handed down by brother Leo

as he passed through East Weymouth, Mass., on the way
to us. How I wondered what that tiny satchel held,
at most a clean shirt plus sox and shorts.
No shaving kit,

my razor dulled on his whiskers each morning.
It wasn't books to read, either. I lent him all
my espionage novels, held an inch from his nose
through the night—judging by the light

under his door—using NHS eyeglasses provided
by Her Majesty. Perhaps he lugged dreams for
a next novel of genius, guaranteeing
riches to restore a lost life.

ASHES TO ASHES

A ten-month wait for
brothers   son   friends
but now's the day
to crack the urn
and spread your ashes
while wife and daughter
stand on slopes above.

Bald rector bare-headed
knee-deep in calm
beyond the rocks,
pants rolled up
collar askew,
intones the ritual
then upends your life into
Chatham Harbor.

Sea sweeps essences of you
your rakish laughter
under a simmering sunset
to tracks of white.

GOODBYE

How was I to know you wanted your last meal,
a last J&B, with me? How much more
I'd have added to whatever we said
eating together in the dormer
upstairs at Christian's,

you watching out the window, gazing up
Main Street eyes fixed on the distance seeing
something I couldn't. Once past your 78th you felt
better and I dared travel. When I got back you
were waiting on my porch. I ought to have suspected.

Wanted an early dinner, a cocktail forbidden
by medication. You finished off fish and chips
to the last French fry, all the while glancing outside
looking, looking. Wondering what you were looking for,
I did peer out the window seeing nothing. How was I to know

you had been making the rounds all week? Happy for
an hour that's sure, then drove home through the fog to
your love, my words in your ear, lay down beside
her before your heart heaved a sigh and died
on a full belly after your first drink in a year.

ODE TO AL

Downpour all the way to Mansfield.
      Over coffee Gussie reveals
            his polished granite stone
                is newly placed.

The beach he loved etched on front.
      NONNO 1921–99 chiseled in back.
            Gleaming slab reflecting hardness an Italian
                grandfather's softness buries deep.

Gone twelve months,
      you stand puzzled at
            how to measure lives,
                perhaps with ten thousand cups

black as this glistening block.
      Maybe with tales told easy
            tongues hot from J&B after
                good days plumbing life.

Perhaps in time he'll fade,
      round face and twinkling eye.
            Bald dome that keeps rolling into view,
                the light he left behind.

HOMELESS SLIM

Lived in woods, the lot next door.
Couldn't avoid him when mowing or collecting my mail.
Accosted with chatter, I'd walk on ignoring him.
Another time close-up, with no booze breath,

he tucked a five-dollar bill in my shirt pocket
saying *You keep a nice place here.*
Showed me a frayed letter from mother
in Brockton, signed *I love you son—Mom.*

Had nothing, not even a last name,
no roof no friends. Clothed in rags and rumors.
A wino 'Nam Vet disabled retarded no one knew.

Gave me a can of Coke as I mowed
one hot day. I dared not drink it. Not notable,
he's maybe five foot five. Spouted nonsense

for two weeks after checks came. Then talked
a sort of sense after cash ran out. Born
like me with parents who had dreams for him.

Found face down in the pond on the corner.
Tossed like a sack of flour in the back of the EMT van.
Anyone know this guy?

FANTASY

A statuesque older woman
penniless and ailing
living with a listless cat

favors dazzling jewelry
stunning gowns
crimson wigs

bought at thrift shops. She
persists in writing poetry and
embracing flights of fancy.

Polly's favorites—

> A very dry Skye
> Martini
> three olives.

> Chinook salmon wild not farmed
> poached in Dom Perignon
> on a bed of wilted greens,

> followed by fruit and fromage
> finished with a rich gelato
> in crystal goblets

—shared with Prince Charles.

TRAGEDY

Bertha left behind
no words we know of
not a letter of love nor
note reminding or
scrap of shopping list

so that laments
or remonstrance
or perhaps correction
spoken in life linger but
in recollection.

Then these too
disappear
such deathly silence
after
so much song.

LONG TREK

Mother crawls along
the New Jersey turnpike
to Baltimore
to greet births of granddaughters
Lois then Loraine

at Johns Hopkins Hospital.
Her spaniel and
journal are seated right
ready for poems
to write themselves.

Always writing
always the poet
why wasn't she killed
mid-metaphor
happily creeping along?

Or grandsmothering
adoring infants at her pinnacle
not decades later
chattering drivel after, long after,
the muse deserted her.

WINTER SQUIRREL

Sunny but cold,
hard
surviving weather,

the feeder aflutter
with blackcaps, purple finch
red crests and tufted tits,

elbowing, scolding,
to spill some seed and soar,
returning to the fray again

while beneath the flailing
a plump and gray tranquility
picks the best that drops from heaven.

OYSTER BAY

Snow-fringed water tidally still,
shrubs shrouded in white.
Bursts of birdsong break the calm

like children safe under snow-quilt
forsythia. Heedless of frost,
they gossip of warmth afoot as

winter shrinks from high sun.
Shoots and buds affirm
they'll live to breed and bloom.

STARRY NIGHT

Dawn of success is but an imitation
    of life streaming in your window.
        Caught in the act, cowardly cloud, you
            leave a wake of disorder, shaking fist,

dying too soon, frothing at the mouth,
    moaning defiance at a world that won't
        work your way. Once done, you skulk
            quickly off to the east, brim

pulled low. Sun sets slowly then
    drops off the edge—it takes
        years to die. Daughters
            look on with a love that can't save

while you drain life
    from them with a last breath.
        Dusk cloaks their pink cheeks,
            stars blinking in their eyes.

FIRST LIGHT

Late fall awakening—dark—no scent—
      flowerless after first frost kill. Birdless
          but for little song of finch and very tiny
             flutter of frigid wings.

Dawn's heat awakens the willow, its gnarls
      releasing creatures from night's crevices.
          Red-winged blackbird ghosts through limbs
             without sound, swooping

through remembrance leaving red streaks
      of fear behind. A tiny creature sits before me,
          a mantis praying. Notice the hands, notice
             the posture. Try to emulate her on those

days when my own prayers for inspiration
      go unanswered and maybe, just maybe,
          the two of us working together can
             move mountains.

INCONVENIENCES

Home at three a.m., aching to hit the sack
feel the mattress seduce and ease into the pillow
when a poem pops to mind. Can't close my eyes
until flipping open the journal and jotting . . .

Like the time *it* pops up at the senior prom
dancing with Lulu, hottest number in the class.
She could raise one—a stiff one—talk about awkward.
I dance apart and talk a lot, but *she knows.*
Guys always raised one dancing in those days
but no more, don't know why . . .

Or the flat tire I get parking with gorgeous Joan
with only five minutes left before I told her dad
I'd have her home. Fifty minutes to mount the spare
but try telling that to her old man with his crooked grin.
But he never notices her sweater inside out . . .

How about when the car quits the other side of Dedham.
Barb and I walk miles for a cab. High heels hurt so bad she
never goes out with me again. And the cabbie stiffs
me twenty bucks when I'm making seventy-five cents an hour
pickin' apples. No more dates that month . . .

GUYS WHO PISS ME OFF

mostly look the same
and always get the girl
like the one in my group
looks like a minister.

Close-trimmed dark hair
clean-shaven with a wide smile
fresh shirt buttoned down
and glasses always glasses.

Don't trust them. Dick or Stan or Bob.
Too damn smart and slippery.
In a foxhole, you get shot
while they duck,

and always get promoted.
While you sweat or fight or help,
they step up for bright medals
with a sham smile.

COSTS

The five-dollar tip you slip Dick the bartender
after three scotches the first night
makes him your friend every night since
with quick service and long pours.
You think how little it takes to buy him
the price of one drink for crissake.

Then think how cheap you sell yourself sometimes
like when she wants you and jumps in bed naked.
Thinking it's an easy piece you jump in after
then spend the next six months shaking her off.

And there's the time the young teller
cashes your check in a rush.
You don't notice the extra thousand
till counting it late in the day.
She'll lose her job being that short,
so you call. The girl's in tears over the loss.
She whispers, *thank God it was you.*

THE FOOL

This morning in the diner
a beauty sat not ten feet beyond
my coffee chatter looking
so like Lil I nearly spoke
before remembering.

Casual shaggy blond, diamond studs sparkling,
white turtleneck under old raspberry sweater soft
over tan slacks, blue eyes still shining from
under a burden of five teens and the fool
husband who wondered about us.

Since you've been gone
the scent of loss
still lingers.

How Lil mocked me day after day from safe
behind her desk declaring *I'm ready for a*
good affair and how I, who hadn't had one,
ought to have leapt at the chance
—while she lived.

SECOND TIME AROUND

You dash up the stairs to my loft
hardly out of breath
where I wait.

We toast and drink the moment

pleasuring each other under the skylight
lingering quickly

then sit at my table
over coffee and complications
before you run home with your guilt.

HARRY

takes early retirement. What's he doing?
        Same thing, only slower, he says. His spouse
                won't retire. Gives him an allowance and license
                        to bore, and laments she's broke.

He complains of her fancy clothes, but
            boasts of their thirty-six-year marriage *still going*—
                a sure sign it's not. *Never felt the need*
                    to stray, but she's another story,

he accuses. She works with execs leaving
        him behind, all clots and knotted knuckles,
                eyes not quite in focus. He leaps my moat
                      and struts in unannounced. Interrupts

new friends. Drops names of bosses like
        old friends. Commands appearance
            at his castle for
                cocktails at five.

His summons won't bring me running.
        Though we're classmates, the distance
                between us yawns. I'm saved by an invitation to
                a spaghetti supper for the homeless.

SAVIOR

In a slaughterhouse, steers are
hammered between the eyes as they
reach the top of the ramp.

Supposed to drop the animal
to its knees to have its throat slit but often
only gets their dazed attention,

blinking soft brown eyes,
quite disconcerting to the slaughterer.
Do you suppose God, aghast,

will hit me between the eyes
before I destroy myself, then become
distraught if I simply blink and go on.

GROW MORE FLOWERS

The NRA wants to arm
teachers and children.

That way when an intruder
attacks your infant
she lifts her very own UZI
from under a blanket and levels him
just as his grenade blasts her crib.

Better that mornings
be spent on the knees
with the unattainable task
of planting red tulips
in remembrance of each dead

blooming in the valley
where gunfire killed so many.

ACCUSING ALAN

You started screwing early and made
Mary pregnant,
both kicked out of high school.
You began business selling junk.

Buried more stolen cars
than state cops could keep track of
but you bought them off
with cash and insults.

Coffee chums warned me
your gifts always had a hook,
not to buy tires from you
for you'd demand favors in return.

It crushed Mary when she
caught you screwing LouAnn
in your office on Mary's desk,
so rich at last you're out of control.

When LouAnn's husband busted in
you beat him up so badly
he's suing you for everything
and will probably win but I doubt it.

ALAN'S STORY

Don't forget I married Mary
and stayed married
unlike most of you fuckers
who look down your noses at me.

Nobody gave me nothin'.
I worked hard for every dime.
Donate cash to every good cause
for all the good it does me.

And as for those crooked cops—
to get a towing contract I had to pay them off
and when they raised the ante
I told 'em where to go.

Family is all that counts.
My brother was all screwed up
after he killed three pals
piling his car into a tree on Easter.

I supported him till he died
and his family too.

As for the bastard suing me
what's wrong with a little piece
on the side. Suing
won't stop me screwing.

ENDANGERED

Friendly robins in the blue spruce
      outside my window overlooking marsh
            and ocean cry out about a report
                  that humans have driven the pace of bird

extinctions to one hundred times
      the natural rate. My robin hasn't read it but
            agrees to poll some peers. Mornings later
                  from the old oak, loud chirps awaken me

to a chorus of concern. Seems few birds
      read except for a wise waxwing. She has
            a gull bring the report from a dumpster. She
                  recites the situation to my robin,

plus a crow familiar with alarmist news,
      a cardinal known for integrity, plus some
            adaptable sparrows.
                  It seems there is no natural rate of

extinction. From the worldwide flight
      of a dying condor comes
            the wail that humans are
                  disappearing as fast as they.

LOIS AND DA

Lois surprises me on Father's Day with a warm card and
an 8x10 Polaroid of her and my father. Nineteen
and into pot she's named her Doberman *Panama Red*
in honor of what she smokes. She stares
because she's high, but I who took the picture
have no clue that *Panama Red* is anything but a dog.

Sitting on a love seat with my father, she wears a summer
dress. His attire as always is a suit—
white-shirt-tie—his rumpled academic look. English
professor and writer, he's seventy, hasn't worked in years
and lives in England off his second wife, Jean. My Da lands
penniless at Logan each summer expecting me to feed
and drive him to see his aged mother. We worry

she'll die before he next returns. He brings
Nana's favorite marzipan. The rest of us are compensated
with conversation. I can listen
for hours as he rhapsodizes on Britain's faded glory.
I love my Da
no matter that he failed to support us.

Lois marries in a year, bears two sons and divorces.
Nana dies at one hundred and four, outlived by her son
by only six years. He dies in Jean's arms in glorious England.
Jean, who pours cold water over him when *she's* angry.
In that blessed photo, my ignorance is innocence.
Anger at my father is absent.

LOIS AT HER FARMSTAND

A small log home atop
a hill of cleared acreage
is backdrop to love's sweat.
Second husband Doug nearby
works even on Sunday inventing
ways to turn a dollar crushing glass
with his new dump truck.

My daughter evolves
from suburban rebel to farm wife
rebel years but a bad dream
clothed in print dress
shit-kicker boots
and local patter for the lady selectman
who wants *today's* tomatoes.

So complete so confident
after awful years of estrangement.
The miles I came to find her
are nothing against the journey
she's endured to find herself.

PARENTING

That day on the docks at Annapolis
I held you, an infant, in my arms

fearful of your frailty and my dominion
as you hung suspended over water

with nothing but me, the frail one,
to keep you, the strong one

who survived to fly,
from drowning if you dropped.

LORAINE-WALKING

A ritual—to slip out early before
  others wake on Christmas weekend
    to walk the whole year through watching
      full moon spear itself on bare branches

while sun sears its way to day.
  We sweat a last turn. You think out loud
    how easy it'll be once past forty
      with all trials complete and children grown.

From an aged perch my silence
  is wisdom, knowing surface stuff
    wears away too soon, from body heat and
      careless words. When stars go out, vision

pierces fluff and whisks away illusion, exposing
  jagged peaks, dark corners, sharp edges,
    nothing that might mesh with dreams.
      Most might part at this point but a

persistent few—some say foolish—notice light
  within, overcome fears as shadows lessen, angles
    soften until the scary thing called
      love comes soft and round again.

PROVINCETOWN ALLOWS NO BIRDSONG

On Law Street this morning a cardinal
hidden in a maple
broke the rules
and sang.

COPING

Sprint the steps.
Breathe the peaks.
Coast the slopes.

CAPE COTTAGE IN WINTER

In Sagamore center
off Main Street
down a long lane lies
a vacant house cedar concealed
sitting in a saucer

scooped by glaciers,
peering over the edge
with its one-eyed gable,
nudging mansions aside
to spy the sea.

With paint peeling
shutters aslant
and downspouts drifting
this humble bungalow
invites a peek that reveals

tiny white-washed space
crammed to the eaves with books
chipped dishes shelved
wobbly chairs at a scarred table
mother, seated with spaniel, penning a poem.

III

Immortality?
It isn't anything I'd lose sleep over.

— STANLEY KUNITZ

SAGAMORE BEACH

Sunny October afternoon
    standing on stone jetty,
        beach at our backs
            Cape Cod Bay before us.

The ribboned box I hold
    contains your ashes. Richard
        holds yellow roses he's brought.
            You're walking the beach with

spaniels Eloise and Honey.
    Both sons here as you asked,
        along with my Linda, friend Geoff,
            young Todd, your faithful Lilla.

All the rest are with you—
    spectators that we sense.
        Lilla brought two of your poems
            for Richard to read. I read two

of mine you might like. You're
    picking up driftwood for a cottage
        fire. I try to tell you the cottage is gone.
            You already know. Richard opens

your ashes—startling snow white—
    and pours them downwind. Linda
        passes out roses to toss after ashes.
            Current floats them south,

alongshore toward the canal.
    We voice thoughts of you,
        gaze after roses drifting
            out to sea. You, unhurried,

pace your roses, far off and fading.
      I wave. You wave back and turn
            to walk away with your one love,
                  holding hands, deeply, lastingly

in love, excluding all else. You, Patsy and Paul,
      bore us babes back when the Great Depression
            swept away dreams. Only letters live to
                  speak of your love to us, your sons.

COMMUNION

You barge
into her solitude—
a great blue heron.
Stop.
Stare
and part in peace.

She continues
with silent strides
her arch-necked prayer.

You resume
a bog-side stroll—
richer.

ONE FIFTEEN P.M.

On Thanksgiving
we're about to sit down
when the call comes
answered upstairs to escape
the sounds of revelry.

It's my only brother
not heard from since July.
She just died he whispers as if
afraid of waking his wife.

I tell him I love him
four times I think.

The fireplace crackles.
A tufted titmouse flits
to the feeder.

JUMP

Learning early to jump,
        my tortures toughened me
                for poems that lay hidden.

Guys my age seldom have
        this chance. I've seen the Roman Coliseum
                and it's awesome.

I cross my street, running
        to the sound of stars cracking
                horizons falling away, a ticket to anywhere.

In full-color shit blood and black stripes
        streaks past the finish line
                feet not even touching ground.

We sweat the last turn. You
        think out loud how easy
                it will be once past forty.

THREE SPRING HAIKUS AFTER SURGERY

Night Nor'easter

Gale winds exhausted
from rattling my skylight go
off to sleep at dawn.

Spring Snow

Powdery frosting
layers a wedding cake scene,
hiding crocuses.

Storm Morning Lighthouse Beach

Growling angry sea,
white-toothed waves snap at the wind,
froth in frustration.

A COUPLE OF COLD ONES

Emerging from surgery
my throat parched,
Carl's elfin smile
offers my new knees
a couple of cold ones.

Delirium surely,
he doesn't drink
and I'm on Coumadin.

After he leaves
the nurse inspects
his generous gift—two quahogs on ice.

IDLE THOUGHTS WHILE HEALING

New Day

Dawn blushes
before dropping
her robe.

Black-capped Chickadee

Fearless acrobat, half-ounce
of black and white sass,
tiny buxom zest

flits to the feeder
braving giants offering
sunflower seed.

Day's End

Moonlight bathes
a bedroom, washing worry
from the sleepers.

Poets

Weaving small truths
endure to survive
the largest lies.

ARNOLD'S AXIOM

Integrity's the only thing I can't teach you, spoken
that first fall morning surveying in South Walpole as he

passed his belt through the loop on the end of a steel tape,
gave me the handle and turned the way my scope pointed.

Notebook in one hand, brush-hook in the other,
slashing through saplings, shouting over his shoulder,

keep me on line—
going in the right direction.

I laugh.

at me, seventeen, keeping Arnold on line.
No more words survive, yet ever since

he's kept me mostly honest.

He believes his poet-daughter led
me astray toward poetry.

Integrity's the only thing I can't teach you.
Integrity—the only thing I learned.

THOUGHTS ON A WEDDING IN PROVINCETOWN

Me rejoicing amid five friends
three bouquets two boutonnières
and sprays of blooms on a pedestal
recalling the ways I squandered myself.

Astonished to be in this place
after sentencing myself to any one
of a dozen prior deaths,
frivolous to prestigious to

bankrupt.
One or all could have been fatal.
How can one who errs so
often be so blessed

with lover, daughters and friends?
No doubt my torments
taught me to want
the poems that lay ahead.

BAGEL AND COFFEE AT 6 A.M. ON MACMILLAN WHARF

Sitting lonely, away a week,
the shoreline curves toward home
an hour south under a steel quilt sky lifting
its silver hem to show a day's hope,

where you awaken warm and alone, you
who redeemed me after the joke
of a life I led waking with lovers I fled
for lack of morning words.

Nearby sagging tenements shelter
Rumanian blondes made rich at
minimum wage
serving fruit smoothies.

Beggar sparrows are eclipsed by
a soaring black-backed gull.
The wharf's foul fish stink redeemed
by the sea's sharp tang.

It's time to go home.

OLD COLONY TAP

Tables and bar ripple with carved scars.
Smoke hovers like an apparition
from damp Camels fisherfolk smoke.

Fred weaves drunk perched on an end stool,
back to the wall to stay upright then
dies next month toppling from his boat.

Ken clad in filthy plaid and foul mouth
shouts love at Lulu still chesty at fifty.
Both freeze in the next blizzard.

Gentle Ozzie all alone, gray curls on the bar,
dreams off a drunk, yearning to give his life
to a drowning boy off Race Point.

These wraiths are real, though
dead. I'm not real, no better than
they. Ancient taps in this quaint town.

AGING

Do you remember our Alsatian
leaping snowdrifts
paws pumping through snow
pretending youth
with Samson
the Great Dane pup
sleeping for two days after?

Like us this morning
romping through
new purple percale
three-hundred-count
love exceeding our ages
worth a week's exhaustion
as we laugh still at the thought
of two dogs long dead
cavorting in life
just like us.

SPRING HOPE

Around the corner of my eye
swoops a golden finch to
alight on an ancient apple,
branches in full bud.

       Her symphony bursts
       to belie the tiny shape

Our songs embrace no dark.
All is life

       death but
       the small space between.

GONE TOO LONG

Hi grampa
this is Peter
glad I came
most guys my age
never have this chance.
I've just seen the Acropolis
and it's beautiful
our roots are here you know.

He speaks from a card-fed phone
beside iridescent Aegean
seven hours time difference
from Cape Cod
harbored in history
alongside berthed triremes
that sank a Persian fleet
before Christ lived.
His ship
the SS *Massachusetts*
on a training cruise,
his home for a long fifty days
squats dockside
dwarfing ancestors
in comfort speed and safety.

He of the power plant
learning the sweat of steam
instead of oars and sails
still longs for home as I do.

ABLE SEAMAN

In his fifties
sturdy frame
maybe five feet six
salt-and-pepper hair cropped short
warm in heavy anorak
over blue shirt open
gray slacks well-worn
black shoes thick soles.

Lunch sausage with a pint
eaten on watch as eyes squint
then lick a cigarette
just rolled
held in hardened hands
with a touch oddly delicate
draws hard to catch the spark.

Holding horizon and folk in focus,
Michael returns always to this wharf
catching the ebb without a word
calming his seas.

CROSSING OVER

I cross my street alone
blackness on the far side of the mountain,
a new day ushered in
by the yip and yowl of coyotes
the sound of stars cracking
horizons falling away
my plane ticket to anywhere
without heartbreak.
Scars rub themselves out
a new form of hush.
Clear-eyed I collect free samples you said
I could have when I was grown-up
though I knew I'd stay a child
would always be a child
forever and ever
like my parents.

TRIUMPH: BOSTON MARATHON, APRIL 15, 1996

Uta Pippig's losing.

Cramps bloody period diarrhea
red and brown streak her legs
sweat mats blond hair
face drains white as she runs past
less than two miles to go
thirty seconds behind.

Ahead a black Kenyan beauty glistens,
topping Kenmore rise in triumph.
Yet Tegla Loroupe doesn't win
the Boston Marathon
on that warm April Monday.

Uta wins.

Tuesday's *Globe* pictures her
in full-color shit blood and black stripes
streaking past the finish line. Shoes
not even touching ground. Hair
in disarray but smiling,
a tired Tegla far behind
watching Uta leap over
the Hancock building.

. . . I was flying.
I think it was the crowd . . .
to win with the little problems I had.

CAPE COD

Knew not a soul arriving here
tired to the bone by lies
ready for a nesting place
tight by ocean
where surf ties sea to sand
with tidal flats fermenting scents

luring bird or winded stranger
to walk a wild and
friendly place
on paths abiding new
restored by clamming days
kindnesses and calm.

DAY'S END IN PROVINCETOWN

Beach baskers
drift off to mandarin martinis
denuding the shoreline.

Scarlet Jeeps
plow scars in the sand.
A crow,

beak crammed with treasure,
lands on a post,
staring at me like I'm the thief.

Walking Commercial Street, a
shout of *Peter!* Friends! Melanie, Molly
and Sam in his stroller.

An island of certainty in a sea
of riptides. Voices and bright
hues scream around us.

DELIVERANCE

Zap me daddy mommy too
treat me sweet with talent
show me how to breathe.

Poems plays and woodcuts too.
Storied tales of how you two
painted lives of not-to-be.

Candles flaring bright but brief
beloved yet doomed, you
let me sip your flame.

Were you puzzled daddy-o
to see your son chase dollars?
It wasn't what you taught me

in six years of art and words
inside a hovel full of love.
Did I baffle you old man?

You thought you got it wrong
risking way too much
before your heir drew breath at fifty.

DID I MAKE A DAUGHTER-DIFFERENCE?

December 22nd
a call from Gilmanton, New Hampshire.
Lois planning Christmas
with sons Peter and Michael says
You know Dad I'm more fortunate than many.

February 19th
driving to the Concord Theatre
after an evening play rehearsal
to pick up teen Stephanie, Loraine
remarks *I am really lucky with my life Dad.*

BE QUICK

This is Patsy's boy
        hard labor freed my mind
                as a gulag
                        spawns great poets.

Prune a twisted cherry bent to earth.
        When stripped
                of strangling vines
                        there's still a spring of life left.

A rabbit fattens on clover
        yards from his burrow,
                feasting at risk or
                        hungering in safety.

When seduction was the limit
        of my talent, I clutched at strangers
                around me. Now I awaken blessed,
                        even on bad days.

Always,
        with thoughts,
                as with strawberries,
                        the wildest are sweetest.